# DATE DUE

|  |  |  |  |
|---|---|---|---|
|  |  |  |  |
|  |  |  |  |
|  |  |  |  |
|  |  |  |  |
|  |  |  |  |
|  |  |  |  |
|  |  |  |  |
|  |  |  |  |
|  |  |  |  |
|  |  |  |  |
|  |  |  |  |
|  |  |  |  |
|  |  |  |  |

# M O T H S

Published by Smart Apple Media

123 South Broad Street

Mankato, Minnesota 56001

Copyright © 1999 Smart Apple Media.

Photos: William T. Hark (cover, pages 2–3, 8–9, 11–12,

21, 23, 27); Entomological Society of America/Ries

Memorial Slide Collection (pages 13–14, 16–19, 22, 24–25,

28–30); Whitney Cranshaw (pages 15, 20); Howard

Ensign Evans (pages 6–7); Dave Leatherman (page 10)

Design &Production: EvansDay Design

Project management: Odyssey Books

**Library of Congress Cataloging-in-Publication Data**

Richardson, Adele, 1966–

Moths / Adele Richardson.

p. cm. – (Bugs)

Includes bibliographical references and index.

Summary: Describes the habitat, life cycle, behavior,

predators, and unique characteristics of moths.

ISBN 1-887068-36-8 (alk. paper)

1. Moths—Juvenile literature. [1. Moths.] I. Title.

II. Series: Bugs (Mankato, Minn.)

QL544.2.R535  1998

595.78–dc21                              98-14619

First Edition   9 8 7 6 5 4 3 2 1

# MOTHS

Adele D. Richardson

*It's summer*. THE AIR IS WARM AND THE SUN IS **BRIGHT**. NEARBY IS A PLANT WITH LEAVES THAT APPEAR HALF EATEN. A CLOSER LOOK REVEALS CATER-PILLARS *nibbling* AWAY AT THE PLANT'S LEAVES AND STEMS TO SATISFY THEIR *ravenous* HUNGER. LATER THAT NIGHT

AT A NEARBY HOUSE, SEVERAL MOTHS

*flutter* MERRILY AROUND A DIM PORCH

LIGHT. THESE TWO INSECTS MAY LOOK

COMPLETELY DIFFERENT, BUT THEY ARE

BOTH A PART OF THE SAME FAMILY. SO

WHAT IS THE CONNECTION? HOW COULD

THEY **POSSIBLY** BE RELATED?

# The Moth's Family

Moths are the nighttime version of butterflies. They both belong to a group of insects called the *Lepidoptera*. The name comes from two Greek words: *lepis*, which means "scale," and *pteron*, which means "wing." This family was so named because of the tiny, powdery scales that cover their wings.

## Differences Between Moths and Butterflies

Moths and butterflies resemble each other in many ways, but there are some important differences. Moths, for example, are NOCTURNAL, and usually come out to fly only at night. Butterflies are DIURNAL, which means they come out to feed and fly during the day, and rest at night.

*The antennae of a male cecropia are large and feathery, not long and slender like a butterfly's.*

You can also tell them apart by looking at their ANTENNAE, or feelers. Butterfly antennae are slender with little "lumps" on the end. Moths do not have these lumps. In fact, a lot of moths have antennae that look like little feathers.

Take a look at the wings of the insects to tell which group they belong in. Most moths have a FRENULUM on their wings. The frenulum acts as a tiny hook and connects their front wings to their hind, or back, wings. Butterflies have no frenulum.

*Eyespots, like these on the polyphemus, are used to scare away hungry predators.*

## Sizing Up

Moths also come in many sizes. Some, like the Giant Hercules moth *(Coscinocera hercules)* of Australia, have a wingspan of about 12 inches (30.5 cm). The WINGSPAN is the distance between the tips of the wings when they are spread apart. The wingspans of the smallest moths, called leafminers, are only about 1/8 inch (3 mm).

*Where Moths Live* There are over 100,000 SPECIES, or types, of moths, and they can be found everywhere in the world except in the oceans. Moths tend to live in warmer climates, like the tropics. This is because they need warm air for their flight muscles to work properly. But not all moths live in warm areas. Some have been found on ice caps in the frozen Arctic. These moths have to "heat up" their muscles before they fly by quickly fluttering their wings.

*This webworm moth uses its proboscis to snack on sweet nectar.*

# The Moth's Family

Like all insects, moths have six legs and breathe air. Their bodies are divided into three main sections: head, thorax, and abdomen.

*Head* The head of the moth is where the most important sense organs are located. Here are its eyes, mouth, and antennae. Moths have two large eyes, one on each

side of the head. These eyes have many separate lenses that help the insect spot movement, like that of a hungry predator.

The two antennae stick out from between the moth's eyes. These are what moths use to smell with. The antennae are very sensitive. For example, the female moth sends out special chemicals, called PHEROMONES, into the air to attract a mate. A male moth can use its antennae

Moth wings are connected to the insect's thorax. Can you see the veins that support this oak worm's wings?

to smell these chemicals from as far as 5 miles (8 km) away!

A moth's mouthparts are on the lower part of its head. Moths that eat (not all do) suck in food through a long, hollow tongue called a PROBOSCIS. This is used to feed on the nectar of flowers and the juice of fruit. When the moth is not eating, the proboscis is coiled up neatly under its face.

**Thorax**   The middle section of a moth's body is called the THORAX. This is where the legs and wings are located. An adult moth has three pairs of legs. On the end of the legs are organs that allow them to taste. Can you imagine tasting with your feet?

Each of the moth's wings is formed by membranes covered with tiny scales that give the wings their colors and patterns.

An adult cecropia rests on a tree branch waiting for night to fall.

The membranes are supported by strong, hollow tubes called VEINS.

**Abdomen**    The last section of a moth's body is the ABDOMEN. Here is where the insect's digestive and reproductive organs are found. The insect also breathes with its abdomen through tiny holes called SPIRACLES. These holes are all over the abdomen and lead directly into the respiratory system.

*This Royal Walnut moth shows off its large abdomen, where it breathes and digests food.*

# Life Cycle of Moths

Moths go through four stages of development during their lifetime. This process is called METAMORPHOSIS, which means "complete change of form." The stages are egg, larva, pupa, and adult.

***Eggs Are Tiny*** Female moths, depending on their species, will lay anywhere from a few to several thousand eggs, usually in the summer or fall months. The eggs are very small—less than .04 inch (1 mm) across—

*The babies inside these tiny eggs will go through two more stages of development before becoming adult moths.*

and are deposited on the types of plants that the young will eat. Moth eggs usually take only about a week to hatch.

**Larva Is Called Caterpillar**   In the second stage of metamorphosis we see the connection between caterpillars and moths.

Caterpillars, called LARVAE (*larva* is singular), are the young, which break out of moth (and butterfly) eggs. They are very small and very hungry, and eat leaves, wood, hair, and even other larvae! Many caterpillars are green from all the plants they eat.

## Long Bodies

The caterpillar's body is made up of a head followed by 13 body SEGMENTS, or sections. The first three segments each have a pair of permanent legs. Farther down the body are five pairs of PROLEGS, which are soft, fleshy legs that will disappear in the next stage of development. These prolegs are used to support the caterpillar's long body. If you've ever seen a caterpillar walk, you can understand why it needs all those legs.

*Many caterpillars have green skin because of all the plants they eat. It won't be long before this plant is gobbled up.*

***Caterpillar Silk*** Just below the caterpillar's mouth is the SPINNERET. This is where the silk comes from. The silk is produced in a stream of liquid that hardens quickly. Silk helps the caterpillar hang on to leaves and branches.

Most caterpillars grow to their full size in about a month. During this time they MOLT, or shed their skin, four or five times. This happens because the insect grows so fast that its skin cannot keep up with its body size. Its old skin will split and the caterpillar will simply wriggle out of it wearing a new, softer skin. Have you ever found an old caterpillar skin?

*The Pupa* After the final molt the caterpillar is ready for the third stage in its development. The process is called PUPATION. During this stage the caterpillar will spin a silk cocoon around its body for protection. Some species will fasten the cocoon to a twig or a rock. Others will simply hide by burrowing into the ground or under leaves and then grow a protective skin called a CHITIN SHELL.

Whether it's inside a cocoon or a chitin shell, once the caterpillar has a protective covering, it becomes a pupa. Now big changes occur. First, most of the caterpillar's old body dies. It is attacked by the same juices that the insect uses to digest

food while in its larva stage. Once the old body is nearly destroyed, the new one of the adult moth begins to take shape. The pupation period can last anywhere from a few days to several months, depending on the species of moth.

---

**Adult Moths Have Short Lives** After pupation is complete, the adult moth breaks out of the protective shell. Most, but not all, moths have wings. Those with wings pump blood into them to make them expand. Soon the adult moth flutters off to search for a mate. Adult moths will live a few days or a couple of weeks, depending on the species, so they must find mates quickly and start the next generation of moths. The adult moths that live only a

*A newly formed adult polyphemus stretches its wings after crawling out of its cocoon home.*

*Spinning a cocoon is hard work, but well worth the effort. When finished, the cocoon will protect the defenseless pupa.*

# Hidden Moths

During the day, moths can fly away from many predators. But how can they protect themselves at night? No problem! Because of the coloring on their wings, most moths can CAMOUFLAGE themselves, or blend in with their surroundings. When at rest they may look just like tree bark or plant leaves. This will trick the hungry predator into sensing that the moth isn't really there.

few days either don't have mouthparts or are so busy finding mates that they don't even eat!

***Moth Self-Defense*** Moths face many predators. Birds, spiders, frogs, and even bats like to snack on these nighttime insects. Some species of wasps are also moth predators. The females will lay their eggs on, or if they can, inside, the moth caterpillars. The body fluids of the caterpillar are food to these growing insects. Eventually, this becomes too much for the caterpillar and it dies.

A moth also protects itself by imitating other insects. For example, it makes a sound that confuses some bats that like to eat it, sending the signal that it doesn't taste very good. The moth makes this sound by rubbing its legs together, or by rubbing its wings against its thorax or abdomen.

Some moths have patterns on their wings that look like the eyes of bigger animals. These are sometimes enough to scare a predator away.

A few species of hawk moths (family *Sphingidae*) are able to beat their wings so

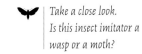

Take a close look. Is this insect imitator a wasp or a moth?

fast that they can be mistaken for bumblebees or hummingbirds. Have you ever seen a moth act like another insect?

---

*Migration*   Many moth species MIGRATE, or move, during the course of their lives. They migrate to find food, mates, or a good place to lay eggs. One Australian species, called the Bogong moths (*Argrotis infusa*), gets away from the summer heat by migrating to the mountains. Because food is hard to find, they enter a resting state called DISPAUSE. In the fall, they "wake up" and head back down the mountains to find mates.

Most moths will migrate as adults

before they mate. This is so the females don't have to carry a heavy load of eggs with them on their trip.

Scientists don't know how moths find their way when they migrate. Some scientists believe that moths can detect and use the earth's magnetic field to determine direction. Others believe they use the position of the sun and moon to plot their course.

How about you? Could you get to the store by just looking at the moon and not using landmarks like buildings and street signs?

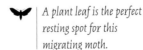 *A plant leaf is the perfect resting spot for this migrating moth.*

 *The white-lined sphinx moth pretends it's a hummingbird while feeding on flower nectar.*

# Friends or Foes

Adult moths actually do no damage. It is their young, the caterpillars, that chew away at plants, fruit, and clothing. Most people think of these insects as worms instead of moth babies. Have you ever pulled a sweater or a blanket out of a closet and found it full of holes? This may well be due to the clothes moth.

There are two types of common clothes moths. One is the case-making moth (*Tinea pellionella*). It is so named because the young spin a case, or shelter, made of silk mixed with tiny pieces of the materials they eat.

The other type is the webbing clothes moth (*Tineola bisselliella*). It earned its name because of the webs it

*A beetle attacks a defenseless caterpillar. Who will win the battle?*

spins all over a piece of material. These young eat clothing because it often contains hair, which is part of their diet. Wool, for example, is made from sheep hair, so it's naturally a food that the caterpillar likes to eat.

These household moths have an adult life of only one to two weeks, mainly because they don't eat once they are all grown up. The female begins to lay eggs on the same day she becomes an adult. Before she dies she will produce around 100 eggs, which she places very lightly on a piece of fabric. Most materials that are moved or shaken regularly will not become moth infested.

 *This larva of the yellow-spotted sphinx moth is well hidden on the underside of a leaf.*

*Helpful Moths* Fortunately, most species of moths are not pests. Many moths are even helpful. For example, the silk cocoons from some moth caterpillars are an important part of industry around the world. Their cocoons are unraveled and woven into fine fabrics. The Oriental Silk moth *(Bombyx mori)*, also known as the Silk Worm, has been used in China for more than 4,700 years. In the late 1980s, these insects produced over 74,000 tons (67,273 MT) of silk worldwide. In fact, this species is so valuable that anyone caught trying to smuggle it out of China can be legally executed!

*This helpful moth pollinates flowers every time it stops for a snack.*

## Can Caterpillars Predict the Weather?

There is no real proof, but many people believe that the banded woolly bear *(Pyrrharctia isabella)*, the larva of the tiger moth *(Arctiidae)*, predicts the weather with the red band on its body. A thick band forecasts a mild winter, while a thinner band means bad weather is coming. This may not be very scientific, but it might be fun to keep a record of the woolly bear's band and see just how many times it is right about the weather!

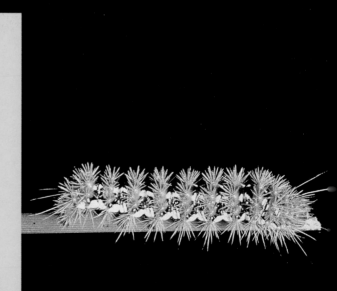

Moths also play an important part in the balance of nature. Not only are they a source of food for some animals, but some species also POLLINATE flowers, as bees do. This happens when a species of moth feeds on the nectar of flowers. Tiny bits of pollen will stick to their bodies and rub off on the other flowers they visit.

# Kinds of Moths

Moths are grouped into different families based on the common physical traits they share. Can you find out which family the moths in your neighborhood belong to?

**All in the Family**  There are about 12,000 species of measuringworm moths (family *Geometridae*). They can be identified by their small bodies and big wings. The Linden Looper (*Erannis tiliaria*) and fall cankerworm (*Alsophila pometaria*) are two types of moths from this family. This is also the family from which the famous caterpillar, the inchworm, comes. Did you know that there is a species of inchworm in Hawaii that can catch and eat flies?

Measuringworms are the second largest moth family. Others have anywhere from a few to several thousand species. Four of the other most common families are described here.

# Owlet and Underwing Moths

This is the largest family of moths, with more than 20,000 species. The scientific name for this family is *Noctuidae*. They are small to medium in size (as far as moths go) and usually have a dull color, like grayish-brown. Two examples of this species are the darling undermoth *(Catocala cara)* and the American dagger moth *(Acronicta americana)*. Most underwing moths have a bit of color, such as orange or yellow, on their hind wings.

On the thorax of these moths is a special organ called a TYMPANUM. The underwings use this to hear the high-frequency sounds made by bats. Once a bat is heard, the moth will fly around erratically, or drop straight down (freefall) to avoid becoming a snack.

# Tiger Moths

Tiger moths (family *Arctiidae*) have over 10,000 species in their family. They are recognized by the bright color patterns on their wings. Two familiar moths from this family are the Isabella moth *(Isia isabella)* and the Great Tiger moth *(Arctia caja)*. The banded woolly bear (the caterpillar that "predicts" weather) also comes from this family. The larvae of some of these moths can eat poisonous plants. The poison will stay in their systems during metamorphosis and cause the adult moths to be poisonous to predators.

# Giant Silkworm Moths and Royal Moths

Luna *(Actias luna)*, Io *(Automeris io)*, and Royal Walnut moths *(Citheronia regalis)* belong to the Giant Silkworm and Royal Moth family *(Saturniidae)*. There are more than 1,300 species in this family. They are recognized by the dark, and sometimes transparent, eyespots on their wings, which they use to scare away enemies. The adults do not eat and will live only a few days after reaching maturity.

# Hawk Moths

Hawk moths (family *Sphingidae*) are also called sphinx moths. Some members of this family include the five-spotted hawk moth *(Manduca quinquemaculata)* and the white-lined sphinx moth *(Hyles lineata)*. There are around 1,000 species in this family, and most have bright colorings. Moths of this family are insect imitators. They are fast flyers and beat their wings so hard that they are often mistaken for wasps, bees, or hummingbirds.

# Learning About Moths

Collecting, mounting, and labeling moths can be a fun hobby. You may even be able to raise some moths and watch the wonder of metamorphosis take place with your own eyes. Or maybe for fun, you can go out into your own neighborhood and try to discover all the moth and caterpillar hiding places. If you're really serious about studying moths, you should keep a record book with you and make note of where you find them as well as what stage of life they are in. Who knows? You may even become a moth expert!

One thing is for sure. Moths play an important role in our world. So go ahead and take a look around. Discover for yourself just how many different kinds of moths live in your own part of the world.

 *Does this moth look familiar? A female cecropia, like the one shown here, could live in your neighborhood.*

## BOOKS

*Butterflies and Moths*, Robert T. Mitchell and Herbert S. Zim, Golden Press, 1977

*Butterflies and Moths*, James P. Rowan, Children's Press, 1983

*Butterflies and Moths Around the World*, Eveline Jourdan, Lerner Publications, 1981

*Butterflies and Moths: How They Function*, Dorothy Hinshaw Patent, Holiday House, 1979

*Caterpillars*, Dorothy Sterling, Doubleday and Company, 1961

*A Closer Look at Butterflies and Moths*, Denny Robson, Gloucester Press, 1986

*Discovering Butterflies and Moths*, Keith Porter, The Bookwright Press, 1986

*Moon Moth*, Carleen Maley Hutchins, Coward-McCann, 1965

*Polyphemus Moth*, Julian May, Children's Press, 1973

*Scaly Wings*, Ross E. Hutchins, Parents Magazine Press, 1971

*Sphinx*, Robert M. McClung, William Morrow and Company, 1981

## CHAPTERS IN BOOKS

*The Big Bug Book*, Margery Facklam, Little, Brown and Company, 1994, p. 11

*Bizarre Bugs: Luna Moths*, Doug Wechsler, Cobblehill Books, 1995, p. 19

*Insect Metamorphosis*, Ron and Nancy Goor, Macmillan Publishing Company, 1990, p. 14

*Insects*, Elizabeth Cooper, Steck-Vaughn Company, 1990

*Weird and Wonderful Insects*, Sue Hadden, Thompson Learning, 1993

## FIELD GUIDES

*The Amateur Naturalist*, Gerald Durrell (naturalist), H. Hamilton Publishers, 1986

*Discovering the Outdoors, a Nature and Science Guide*, American Museum of Natural History, 1969

*Eyewitness–Living Earth*, Miranda Smith, DK Publishers, 1996

*The Living Community, a Venture into Ecology*, S. Carl Hirsch, Viking Press, 1966, pp. 58, 78, 82

*Simon & Schuster Guide to Insects*, Ross H. Arnett, Jr. and Richard L. Jacques, Jr., Simon & Schuster, 1981

## WEB

"Book of Insect Records," University of Florida

"Butterflies and Moths," Department of Entomology, Iowa State University, 1998

"Gypsy Moth in North America," U.S. Department of Agriculture–Forest Service, 1995

"Lepidoptera," Insect Compendium Index, 1997

"Lepidoptera Page," Gordon Ramel (entomologist), 1997

## ENCYCLOPEDIAS

*Academic American Encyclopedia*, Vol. 3, Grolier Incorporated, 1997

*Compton's Encyclopedia* online

*Grzimek's Animal Life Encyclopedia*, Vol. 2, *Insects*, Van Nostrand Reinhold, 1974

*Nature Encyclopedia*, Martyn Bramwell, Warwick Press, 1989

*Nature Encyclopedia*, Checkerboard Press, 1989

*The New Book of Knowledge*, Vol. 2, Grolier, Inc., 1993

*NSA Family Encyclopedia*, Vol. 3, Standard Education Company, 1992

*The World Book Encyclopedia*, Vol. 2, World Book, Inc., 1997

## MAGAZINE ARTICLES

"Obscure Allure," *Natural History*, November 1997, p. 84

"Parasites Looking for a Free Lunch," *National Geographic*, October 1997, p. 74

"Wasp Comeback: Bad News for Gypsy Moths?" *American Forests*, Autumn 1997, p. 6

## MUSEUMS

The Milwaukee Public Museum
Milwaukee, WI

Smithsonian Institution
Washington, DC

Student's Museum, Inc.
Chilhowee Park
Knoxville, TN

Royal Ontario Museum
Toronto, Ontario
Canada

I N D E X